picnics

picnics

FROM HERB LAMB WRAPS TO WILD RICE SALAD

CLARE FERGUSON

jacqui
small

First published in 2006 by Jacqui Small,
an imprint of Aurum Press Ltd,
25 Bedford Avenue, London WC1B 3AT

PUBLISHER Jacqui Small
EDITORIAL MANAGER Kate John
ART DIRECTOR Ashley Western
PHOTOGRAPER Jeremy Hopley
EDITOR Madeline Weston
PRODUCTION Peter Colley

ISBN: 1 903221 64 1

2008 2007 2006

10 9 8 7 6 5 4 3 2 1

Printed in China

contents

INTRODUCTION

Some of my fondest childhood memories involve food eaten out of doors. Even now such activities still delight me. After a long day's work I am often to be found coaxing my husband and friends into joining me for an open-air feast in the local park. Friends may provide some chilled wine or beers. We two will pillage the fridge and storecupboard: snatch olives, cold fish pâté and a crisp cucumber or lettuce. Packed into our baskets will be plates, cutlery, glasses, a corkscrew and paper napkins. In seconds we are off. En route we will pick up a deli-cooked chicken, some crusty baguettes and fresh fruit. When we all meet up at the park, we sit back and breathe a long sigh. Some of the stresses and strains of our lives unravel. Corks fly. Glasses clink. Outbreaks of laughter happen easily.

Care to join me? This book is an invitation to conviviality. Choose your menu from this collection of sumptuous appetisers, soups and hors d'oeuvre, with drinks to match. Or select some sandwiches, roll-ups or wraps for casual eating and partner them with fresh leafy salads. If you intend to impress a crowd, try delicious moist Roast Lamb or Baked Spice Beef – food that you normally eat at home tastes twice as good in the open air. On the following pages you will find all these, along with fresh fruity desserts and frivolous cookies.

Combine, with these, some delicatessen food, breads, cheeses, beers, wines and fruit juice. Not only does this make the planning simpler, but it also makes each meal a unique event. *Picnics* demonstrates a belief in delicious, fresh food, handsomely served. Food must arrive at its destination fresh, safe and undamaged. Advice about how to prepare, pack and present these delicacies is given along with gorgeous colour photographs to inspire you.

Picnics provides ideas for meals, snacks and drinks for those on the move. Enjoy your picnics, wherever they may be. Location is up to you!

Above left: Vacuum flasks come in many styles: stainless steel, plastic and toughened glass or ceramic are all practical.

Above right: A divided lunch box keeps foods separate; stacking plastic tumblers are both safe and space saving.

Opposite, top left: The old fashioned style of ginger beer bottle keeps your drinks secure; carry them in an ice bucket.

Top right: Durable melamine crockery and wooden cutlery are easily transported in a tough plastic shopping bag.

Bottom left: A folding plastic carrying box is ideal for holding all your food containers as well as tumblers and flasks.

Bottom right: Rugs and are throws are an essential for sitting and relaxing.

ESSENTIAL KIT

To keep food or drink in a perfect state of freshness needs some ingenuity and wit, but not necessarily expense. Ordinary household items such as cool boxes, vacuum flasks and jugs, screw-top jars and bottles and snap-top plastic containers can all be utilised. Plastic buckets, bowls or bags; metal or plastic bottle carriers as well as hampers, can be pressed into service. Cutlery, toughened glasses and durable crockery will often fit the bill. But there is also, now, a superb selection of specially designed kit made from colourful, unbreakable plastic, melamine, metal and coated paper. And then there are also the disposable: pretty tumblers, plates, cups, cutlery, napkins made of plastic or paper.

If you are picnicking at dusk, a pressure lamp and lanterns will light your feast. Citronella candles will keep the mosquitoes at bay. Lightweight camping stools will double as tables or stools and are easy to carry.

Don't forget the corkscrew and the rugs and cushions to sit on, and lie back and rest after the feast is over.

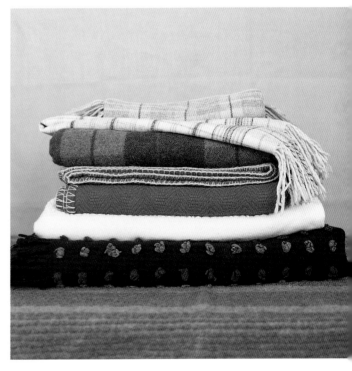

Great picnic food can be easy, quick eaten in the open air. The beach, the

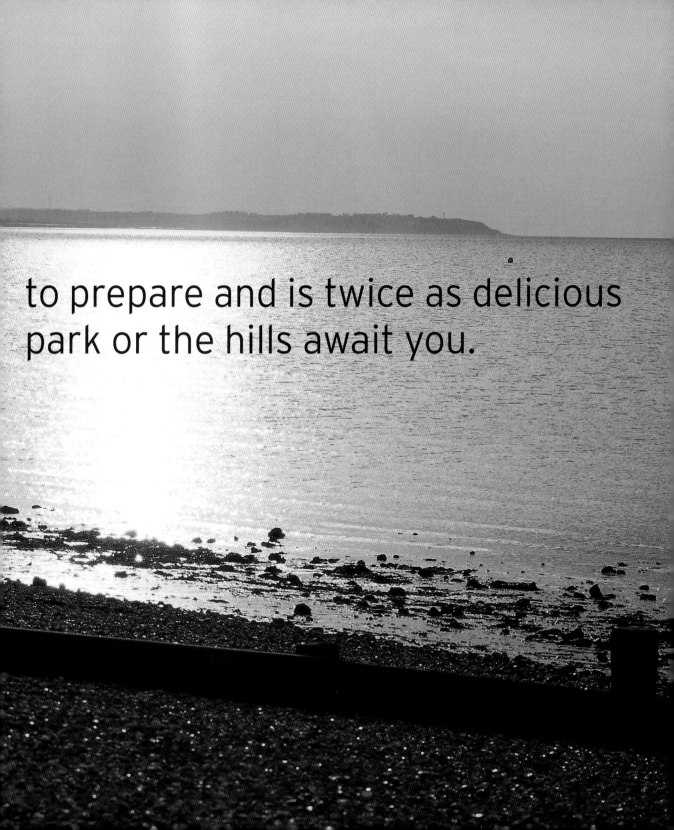

to prepare and is twice as delicious
park or the hills await you.

Left to right: salted almonds, spiced cheese, tapénade

STARTERS & SOUPS

salted almonds

These treats are blissfully simple but very appealing. Once made and completely cold, they'll keep for ages in an airtight jar. They have a satisfying crunch and taste superb at any picnic.

Makes about 500g (about 1 lb 4 oz)

Ingredients
25g (1 oz) citric acid crystals (from pharmacy or specialist deli)
75ml ($\frac{1}{3}$ cup) hand-hot water
500g (4 cups) shelled, unblanched almonds
25g (4 tbsp) table salt

METHOD

1 Toss the citric acid crystals into the water. Stir to dissolve. (If citric acid is unobtainable use the equivalent volume of freshly squeezed lemon juice.) Spread out the almonds in 2 large flat ovenproof trays. Pour the citric acid water over the almonds and leave until well absorbed: about 20 minutes. Drain off excess liquid. Sprinkle the salt over and turn the almonds in it so that they are coated.

2 Bake the almonds, uncovered, in an oven preheated to 180°C (350°F) for 35-40 minutes, stirring twice. Cool on the trays.

3 Once the nuts are cold, spoon them up, shaking off the excess salt, and pack into airtight jars. To transport, take handfuls from the jar and pack into a twist of foil secured with some string. To serve, undo and let people help themselves.

spiced cheese with crudités

Try this spread with crisp, seasonal vegetables cut into sticks: it is hugely adaptable. Chill well before taking on your picnic, especially if on active pursuits.

Makes about 450g (about 1 lb) Serves 8

Ingredients
300g (scant 1$\frac{1}{2}$ cups) curd cheese, cream cheese or low fat soft cheese
50g ($\frac{1}{4}$ cup) salted butter
2 tablespoons hot mustard powder
2 teaspoons hot red paprika
2 tablespoons freshly grated horseradish (optional)
2 tablespoons chopped fresh chives
$\frac{1}{2}$ teaspoon salt
2 tablespoons caraway seeds

Crudités:
Choose from cucumber, (bell) peppers, spring onions (scallions), onion rings, button mushrooms, baby vine tomatoes, carrot and perhaps breadsticks, crispbreads and crackers.

METHOD

1 Cream the cheese and butter together until well blended, and stir in all the remaining ingredients.

2 Pack in individual snap-top boxes, cartons or bowls. Put the selection of crudités in a second, but similar container, ideally rigid, so they stay undamaged in transit.

tapénade with eggs & baguette

Provençale tapénade is a revelation: the flavours sing out at you and it looks dark, glossy and handsome. Surround it with brilliantly yellow-yolked soft-boiled eggs and some torn crisp baguette and you have a feast for eyes, nose and palate. This generous tapénade recipe makes enough for 4 meals: it keeps well in the refrigerator for weeks, though its accompaniments must always be fresh on the day.

METHOD

1 Pit the olives. (Do not even consider using the pre-pitted, water-packed, chemically dyed type: they are a travesty.) Put the olive flesh, the tuna, flaked, and its oil, the anchovies and capers (well rinsed in warm water, twice) and the garlic and thyme into a large mortar or food-processor. Pound using a pestle, or process, in brief bursts, in the food-processor, to a rough black paste.

2 Drizzle in the olive oil, continuing to pound or process, making the paste glossier still. Finally stir in the cognac or brandy. Spoon into a large lidded pot or bowl. Refrigerate.

3 To soft-boil the eggs: allow them to come to room temperature, cover them with hand-hot water, bring to the boil and simmer for 4–5 minutes. Cool under running cold water.

4 Scoop about 50g (2 oz) tapénade per person into the mortar or a pot for transporting. Remove the eggshells and pack the eggs separately.

5 When at the site, halve the eggs crosswise. Slice or tear some baguette. Surround the tapénade with egg halves and bread. Encourage diners to dip the egg into the tapénade and eat, alternating egg with a bite of baguette.

Makes about 675g (1 lb 4 oz) tapénade Serves 16
Presentation serves 4

Ingredients

500g (3½ cups) dry-cured (ideally French) salted black olives
185g (6½ oz) canned tuna, olive oil packed
80g (3½ oz) canned or salted anchovies, drained and chopped
75g (3 oz) pickled or salted capers
5–6 garlic cloves, crushed
2 teaspoons fresh thyme leaves or ½ teaspoon dried
30ml (2 tbsp) extra virgin olive oil
15–30ml (1–2 tbsp) cognac or brandy
4 free-range, organic eggs
1 baguette loaf

smoked trout pâté with celery

Forget those heavy, dense pâtés crusted with butter and laden with fat: this one – made with smoked trout and cream cheese – is as fresh and clean as a new spring day. Make it in minutes and serve in one big, or several little pots. Chill it well or even freeze it briefly before you set out and it will travel in perfect condition.

METHOD

1 Flake the trout into a food-processor or large mortar.

2 Heat the olive oil in a frying pan and sauté the garlic briefly. Add the lemon juice. Spoon this in with the trout and process, or pound using a pestle.

3 Add the soft cheese, paprika, seasonings and some of the herbs and process, in brief bursts, or pound briefly, to make a pink paste, with a slightly rough texture. Taste and adjust seasonings.

4 Smooth into one large or several small, metal containers or china pots. Push a little fresh herb on top of each, and a little extra black pepper.

5 Chill for 1 hour, or refrigerate for up to 4 days. Briefly freeze – say for 45 minutes – if the weather is hot and the journey long. Wash and shake dry the celery. Wrap it in wet kitchen paper or cloth and plastic. Chill it while the pâté chills. Take a knife for spreading.

6 To serve, surround the trout pâté with some crisp, freshly cut lengths of celery.

Makes about 350g (12 oz) Serves 8
Allow 45–50g (2 oz) per serving

Ingredients

250g (9 oz) boneless, skinless hot-smoked trout
1 teaspoon virgin olive oil
2 garlic cloves, chopped
1 tablespoon lemon juice
100g ($\frac{1}{2}$ cup) cream cheese or low fat soft cheese
$\frac{1}{2}$ teaspoons mild paprika
sea salt and freshly ground black pepper
2 tablespoons chopped fresh herbs e.g. dill, chives
2 celery hearts

pork rillettes with endive and rolls

METHOD

1 Remove the pork rind, bones and cartilage, and set aside. Chop the meat into 2.5cm (1 in) chunks. Put the rind, fat side down, in a casserole. Add the meat, bones, cartilage and remaining ingredients. Pour in 100ml ($\frac{1}{2}$ cup) cold water; cover tightly. Bring to a simmer, check, cover tightly again and turn to the lowest possible heat, or put into an oven preheated to 130°C (250°F). Cook for about 3 hours until the meat and fat disintegrate. Do not let the pan boil dry: add a little water as needed.

2 Remove casserole from the heat. Pour pan contents into a sieve over a bowl. Discard rind, bones, cartilage, any other debris such as bay leaves and stems.

3 Using clean fingers, tease apart and shred the solids. Put in a clean bowl. Add enough of the strained fat to create a creamy paste. Smooth the mixture into jars. Drizzle over extra fat, thinly, to seal. Push reserved thyme sprigs into the fat to garnish. Once completely cold, refrigerate. Add lids after several hours of chilling. Take the jars to your site.

4 To serve, let people scoop the rillettes into each split roll and push in some chicory leaves.

Makes about 800g, Serves 8

Ingredients

1.5kg belly pork, including rind
4 garlic cloves
$\frac{1}{2}$ nutmeg, grated (1 teaspoon grated nutmeg)
$\frac{1}{2}$ tablespoons black peppercorns, coarsely crushed
$1\frac{1}{2}$-2 tablespoons sea salt flakes or kosher salt
75g bunch parsley stalks, tied with string
1 sprig (3-4 leaves) fresh bay, bruised
50g fresh thyme sprigs, plus extra to garnish

To serve:

8 crusty bread rolls
1 head chicory (Belgian endive)

green pea & prosciutto soup

Real, fresh baby green peas in the pod are a brief luxury: they must be eaten within hours of picking. This recipe, using easily obtainable frozen petits pois, gives you the sweetness, colour, succulence and vitamins of fresh peas and it can be completed within 20 minutes. Serve it hot or cold, with some mellow cured Italian ham added at the end.

METHOD

1 Heat the butter in a saucepan and when sizzling add the spring onions (scallions) and sliced potatoes. Fry for 1-2 minutes, stirring now and then. Add the peas and boiling water and bring the pan contents back to boiling. Cover the pan, reduce the heat and cook for 8 minutes more.

2 Add half the milk and half the pan contents to a blender. Blend until smooth. Pour out the blended soup. Now, to the blender, add the remaining milk, remaining pan contents and 2 of the ham slices, scissor-chopped. Blend again until the mixture is smooth.

3 Combine the two mixtures, stir, taste and season well. Reheat to boiling once again and pour into wide-mouthed vacuum flask and seal. Alternatively chill completely, then add several ice cubes and pour into the vacuum flask. Wrap the remaining prosciutto in waxed paper.

4 To serve, pour out the soup, hot or cold, into big mugs, china cups or soup bowls. Pass soup spoons. Finger-shred the remaining prosciutto into each serving.

Makes 1.5 litres (6¼ cups) Serves 8

Ingredients

25g (2 tbsp) butter, chopped
6 spring onions (scallions), green and white parts, sliced
50g (2 oz) new potatoes, scrubbed and sliced
750g (6 cups) frozen petits pois
500ml (2½ cups) boiling water
250ml (1 cup) creamy milk
6 thin slices prosciutto di Parma (cured Italian ham)
salt and freshly ground white pepper

hot borscht with rolls or bagels

The best borscht I've tasted was in Moscow; the next best in the Marais, in Paris, but my own is opinionated and tasty. Raw beetroot works best: if unobtainable use cooked beets. Serve this soup with soured cream, crème fraîche or more abstemiously, with low-fat fromage frais. Rolls or bagels are a great accompaniment.

METHOD

1 Combine the oil, garlic, onion, chilli, carrot and mushrooms in a saucepan. Cook, stirring, over a high heat for 2 minutes.

2 Peel, slice or cube the beetroot into the pan then add the boiling stock and most of the vinegar. Bring the pan contents back to boiling. Reduce heat, simmer for 15-20 minutes or until the beetroot is tender and flavours blended. Taste, add remaining vinegar if you like and add salt and pepper to balance.

3 If you prefer a smooth soup, blend the soup to a purée. Pour the hot soup into a wide-mouthed vacuum flask. Seal tightly. Pack the herbs and cream or fromage frais separately in pots with secure lids. Pack cups, mugs or glasses or bowls.

4 To serve, pour out portions of soup. Add a spoonful of cream, soured cream or fromage frais, and sprinkle with fresh coriander (cilantro) leaves. Pass the rolls or bagels and enjoy.

Makes 1.5 litres (6½ cups) Serves 8

Ingredients

1 tablespoon virgin olive oil
4 garlic cloves, chopped or crushed
1 red onion, sliced
⅛-¼ fresh red chilli e.g. serrano, or habanero
1 carrot, thinly sliced
8g (¼ oz) dried mushrooms e.g. ceps or morels, crumbled
600g (1 lb 5 oz) fresh beetroot or cooked canned beets
1 litre (4 cups) boiling chicken stock
2-3 tablespoons red wine vinegar
salt and freshly ground black pepper
handful fresh coriander (cilantro) leaves, to garnish

To serve:

8 tablespoons soured cream, cream or low-fat fromage frais
8 crusty white rolls or bagels

Left to right: cheese, ham and salad-filled mini loaves
crusty breads with spicy peppers and jamon serrano

SANDWICHES

crusty breads with spicy peppers & jamon serrano

A 'bocadillo' is a sandwich – a well-loved snack found all over Spain. The tastes are delightful: the olive oil is invariably fruity and spicy and green; the cured meats superb and the pickles, preserves and beans wonderful. Make these sandwiches and dream of Seville or Bilbao. Drink a classy Rioja or Navarra wine to complete the image.

METHOD

1 Slice the rolls lengthwise almost in two but keep a hinge on each. Drizzle the interior crumb of each base with 2 teaspoons of the oil, almost 3 tablespoons in total.

2 Mash 2 tablespoons of the remaining oil with the white beans, garlic, salt and pepper, to make a messy paste. A fork will do this perfectly well.

3 Spoon a quarter of this bean paste along each roll. Fold in 2 slices of serrano ham to each. Pack 2 or 3 *piquillo* peppers on top. Now wrap each roll in a square of waxed paper or a colourful cloth. Pack into a basket, pannier or bag to transport.

Serves 4

Ingredients
- 4 long bread rolls
- 5 tablespoons extra virgin olive oil
- 250g (9 oz) cooked white beans (canned, or in jars from a good delicatessen)
- 4 garlic cloves, crushed
- salt and freshly ground black pepper
- 8 thin slices *jamon serrano* (Spanish cured, mountain ham)
- 8-12 canned *piquillo* peppers (roasted, skinned, spicy red peppers) or canned pimientos

cheese, ham &
salad-filled mini loaves

Variations of the famous French recipe, pan bagnat, these are masterpieces of invention: fillings packed neatly into crusty rolls or tiny loaves with the top lids and crumb removed. The lid is then set back on top, sealing them for travelling – and they are so durable they withstand rough treatment. To eat they can be sliced into halves or quarters.

METHOD

1 Slice off and keep the lids of each roll. Set aside.

2 Using a grapefruit knife, scoop out the crumbs, leaving an even, crusty wall or shell. Pile the crumbs into a food-processor along with half the olive oil, the pesto and parsley. Process in bursts, to get densely green fragrant crumbs.

3 Use the remaining oil to brush inside each hollowed-out roll, including the interior of the lid. Spoon an eighth of the crumbs into each roll. Add a folded prosciutto slice. Add more crumbs and a quarter of the roasted artichokes or mushrooms and cheese. Push in the second prosciutto slice and 4 olives. Push the lid into place on top.

4 Wrap tightly using waxed paper, plastic wrap or dampened cloth. Wedge them, upright, into a small box or basket.

5 On site, undo the wrappings. Let diners eat them whole, halved or quartered.

Serves 4

Ingredients

4 round or oval crusty rolls
6 tablespoons extra virgin olive oil
4 tablespoons fresh pesto (not pasteurised)
1 handful flatleaf parsley, chopped
8 slices prosciutto di Parma (cured Italian ham)
250g (9oz) canned, roasted artichokes or wild mushrooms in oil, drained
125g (4½ oz) soft blue cheese, e.g. Gorgonzola, Roquefort, Bleu d'Auvergne, Bleu de Bresse
16 dry-cured salted black olives, pitted, or anchovy-stuffed green olives

ham & gherkin roll-ups

Sweet, cooked ham, sharply piquant baby cocktail gherkins and chutney-flavoured butter, all rolled up inside soft white bread makes finger food for children (and the young in heart) which is easy and delicious. These are treats for any occasion: a picnic, tea party, trip to the grandparents, or to take in your back-pack when off on adventures to mountains and lakes. They are also extremely convenient to pack.

METHOD

1 Pile the bread up high. Use a sharp, serrated knife to slice off and discard the crusts. Wrap the bread briefly in a dampened cloth, or spray with water.

2 Meanwhile mix the soft butter with the chutney. Drain and dry the gherkins. If using a large dill pickle, slice lengthwise into 8 segments.

3 Unwrap the bread. Line the slices up in a row. Using a spatula, rubber scraper or palette knife, coat the bread slices with the chutney-butter. Put each bread slice on a square of plastic wrap, and set a ham slice on each. Put 3 gherkins (end to end) or a dill pickle segment diagonally across each ham-covered bread slice.

4 Now, starting at one corner, roll each slice up tightly. Place these, joins down, on the same dampened cloth, in two piles. Wrap up neatly. Pack inside a plastic box or bag. Take a sharp, preferably folding, knife.

5 To serve, cut across, at an angle, giving 16 roll-ups, and remove plastic wrap. Perfect to eat in your fingers!

Makes 16 Serves 4

Ingredients
8 thin slices very fresh white square 'tin' loaf
2 tablespoons salted butter, softened
1 tablespoon mango or other chutney, finely chopped
24 tiny cocktail cornichons (baby gherkins) or
   1 large dill pickle, drained
8 slices cooked smoked ham

crab & ginger sandwiches

I first tasted these, or something similar, at a party. We sipped wine and a waiter carried around a handsome sourdough loaf inside which, like treasures, we found fine, tiny little sandwiches. You can vary the filling (e.g. smoked salmon could be an alternative) but keep the concept similar: it's impressive, portable and certainly a stylish feast.

METHOD

1 Slice off a top 'lid' from the loaf; set it aside. Using a sharp, serrated knife, make a vertical cut, about 1cm (½ in) in from the crust, all the way round and nearly to the base. Cut a line across the centre of the crumb. Using your fingers, carefully lift out a each 'plug' of bread.

2 Trim the bases of these bread chunks to make them smooth. Turn the pieces of crumb flat side down, and, using an electric carving knife or sharp, serrated knife, slice each thinly into 6 or 8 thin layers. Stack in 2 piles and cover with a dampened cloth.

3 Squeeze a little lemon and grate a little zest into the butter. Grate the ginger finely, skin and all. Scrape the pulp into the butter. In a bowl, break up the crabmeat with a fork, add the mayonnaise and seasonings. Beat well until smooth. Unwrap the bread. Butter 2 bread slices and spread on a share of crab filling. Press the sandwich closed.

4 Repeat until all the bread slices are used up, and wrap once again in the damp cloth for 10-30 minutes. Unwrap. Stack the finished sandwiches in the same chunks again, and insert each carefully in the hollow loaf. Slice the sandwiches across, inside the crust, to make quarters, and again to make triangles. Set the lid on top of the loaf as normal. Wrap the entire loaf in plastic wrap or foil.

5 To serve, unwrap the loaf and place on a cloth-covered tray. Allow friends to lift the lid and help themselves.

Serves 8 or more

Ingredients
1 large 'boule' (round shaped) sourdough or whole wheat loaf (about 850g/2 lb)
1 lemon or lime
75g (6 tbsp) salted butter, softened
2.5cm (1 in) piece fresh root ginger, scrubbed
400g (14 oz) prepared, cooked crabmeat, lobster or smoked salmon
3 tablespoons thick mayonnaise or hollandaise sauce
⅛ teaspoon cayenne pepper
sea salt and freshly ground black pepper

prosciutto & treviso wraps

These are a miracle of ease and style: finger food for the great outdoors which appeals to the eye as well as the taste buds. Select crisp, pretty Italian salad leaves. Keep them intact and, on site, roll them up around a twist of fine fragrant prosciutto di Parma, one of the world's most delicious of foods, and some freshly sliced melon (ogen, galia and cantaloupe are excellent).

METHOD

1 Wash the salad head but leave it intact. Leave the prosciutto on its waxed paper, rolled up loosely. Take the whole, washed melon.

2 On site, set out all the components in a cloth-lined hamper or basket and add a pile of plates. Cut the melon, removing skin and seeds, into fine slivers. Participants pull off one or two leaves of radicchio, add a slice of ham, a sliver of melon and a few grinds of pepper. It is then rolled up and eaten.

Serves 4-6

Ingredients

4 heads *radicchio de trevise* or *ceriolo verde* radicchio (red chicory), or 2 of each
12 slices prosciutto di Parma (cured Italian ham)
1 ripe, scented whole rock or musk melon
fresh peppercorns, in a pepper grinder

watercress sandwiches

Somehow these brings to mind childhood simplicity. Who would have thought that a sandwich could combine two different textures so successfully? Ensure that the cress is very clean, the butter at a spreading temperature and the bread soft and these sandwiches can be prepared in a few minutes and enjoyed at any picnic.

METHOD

1 Spread out the bread into two lines, edges touching, so that it makes one rectangle.

2 Whisk the butter with the mayonnaise, and the boiling water: you should obtain a mousse-like cream. Use a wide-bladed spatula or rubber scraper to smooth the butter-mousse across all the bread slices, right to the edges.

3 Shake the cress dry. Pull or snip off the cress sprigs and press them on the buttered surfaces of half the slices so they are well covered. Sprinkle with black pepper to taste. Lay a buttered slice face down on a cress-covered slice; pile up the sandwiches into a tower. Pressing down evenly, use a sharp, serrated knife to slice off and discard the crusts. Leave the sandwiches whole.

4 Use waxed paper, plastic wrap or a wet cotton table napkin to wrap the sandwiches tightly in a neat block. Take the same sharp, serrated knife to the picnic site along with a lettuce, washed and wrapped in dampened cloth or plastic.

5 To serve, unwrap the sandwiches. Slice into four triangles, squares or fingers. Arrange as liked on a plate, basket or tray on a bed of salad leaves.

Makes 24 small sandwiches Serves 4

Ingredients
12 slices thin white square 'tin' loaf
75g (6 tbsp) salted butter, softened
2 tablespoons thick mayonnaise
2 teaspoons boiling water
1 bunch or 2 x 85g (3 oz) packs watercress or cress, washed
freshly ground black pepper
salad leaves, e.g. Webb's Wonder, to garnish

lebanese lamb wraps

In the Middle East lamb *kibbeh* may be presented either raw or cooked. In this version it is cooked and, instead of cracked wheat, I use couscous which adds an interesting texture. Make the *kibbeh* just before you set off, and wrap them in foil to serve hot, or alternatively make them ahead and chill or even freeze them. They still taste excellent defrosted and heated well using a steamer, microwave or moderate oven.

METHOD

1 Mix the lamb, spice mix, celery salt and parsley together. Leave to stand, covered, in a cool place.

2 Mix the couscous with the boiling stock, garlic, lemon juice and, once it has cooled, the mint. Leave until cold. Drain off any excess liquid.

3 Add the lamb, using clean hands, and knead it all well together. Divide into 12. Shape each into a torpedo-shaped *kibbeh*, smoothing off the ends.

4 Cook these in an oven preheated to 180°C (350°F) for 20-25 minutes or microwave them, six at a time, on High (750 watts) for 3 minutes, turning them after 2 minutes. If you prefer, grill (broil) 8-10 minutes, turning, or barbecue about 10 minutes. Pack in foil to remain warm, or allow to cool to room temperature before packing.

5 Take the serving ingredients separately and, on site, wrap each *kibbeh* in a wrap of flat bread, adding some apricot halves, parsley, Cos leaves and a blob, if you like, of ready-made *hummus bi tahini*. Eat in the fingers.

Serves 4

Ingredients
500g (1 lb) twice-minced good quality lean lamb
2 tablespoons spice mix such as Chermoula
1 teaspoon celery salt
1 handful parsley, chopped
100g (²/₃ cup) 'instant' couscous
100ml (scant ½ cup) boiling stock or water
2 garlic cloves, chopped
2 tablespoons freshly squeezed lemon juice
1 handful fresh mint, chopped

To serve:
4 thin lavash flat breads (or roti, pitta or tortillas)
100g (½ cup) pre-soaked, pitted dried apricots
extra flatleaf parsley sprigs
8-12 Cos lettuce leaves (outer ones)
100g (½ cup) *hummus bi tahini* (chickpea and tahini paste) (optional)

garlic- and anchovy-stuffed roast lamb

MAIN COURSES

garlic- & anchovy- stuffed roast lamb

Serves 8

Ingredients

   1 leg spring lamb, about 2.5-2.75kg (5^1/$_2$-6 lb)
   100g (4 oz) canned anchovy fillets, drained and halved
   10 garlic cloves, halved lengthwise
   20 pistachios, skinned and blanched
   2 tablespoons extra virgin olive oil
   freshly ground salt and black pepper
   4 red onions, unpeeled, halved crosswise
   3 tablespoons aged balsamic vinegar
   120ml (^{1}/$_2$ cup) robust red wine

METHOD

1 Pat the lamb dry. Roll an anchovy half round each garlic half and each pistachio. Using a sharp knife make a 2cm (^{3}/$_4$ in) deep cut in the thickest part of the leg. With the blade in the cut, insert an anchovy roll. Do this all over the upper part of the leg.

2 Place the lamb a large roasting pan. Drizzle the oil all over and sprinkle with salt and pepper. Roast in an oven preheated to 190°C (375°F) for 20 minutes per 500g (1^1/$_4$ lb) and 20 minutes over: 2-2^1/$_4$ hours.

3 Roughly 45 minutes before the end of cooking add the onions, cut sides up, all round the roast.

4 When cooked, transfer the lamb and the onions to a portable serving dish. Drizzle the balsamic vinegar over the onions. Leave the meat and its juices to 'set'.

5 Pour off excess fat from the pan and leave the 'jus': stir in the wine. Cook, stirring, to make a thick sauce. Pour it into a sealable container and pack.

6 On site, carve the meat thickly, serving with the onions and the red wine sauce.

stuffed quail

Serves 4

Ingredients

   8 prepared quail or boneless quail
   85g (^{1}/$_2$ cup) seedless muscat raisins
   8 slices prosciutto di Parma (cured Italian ham)
   50g (^{1}/$_2$ cup) toasted pinenuts
   8-16 vine leaves, fresh, or preserved, blanched and drained
   1-2 tablespoons extra virgin olive oil
   6 tablespoons muscat-type wine

METHOD

1 Choose a large, shallow flameproof casserole or a metal baking pan into which the quail fit snugly. Mix the raisins, half the ham, scissor-chopped, and the pinenuts together. Push some of this stuffing loosely inside the cavity of each bird.

2 Wrap a slice of prosciutto loosely around each bird. Set each wrapped bird inside a nest of vine leaves in the casserole or baking pan. Rub or dot each bird with a little oil or bacon fat. Splash the wine over.

3 Bake the birds, uncovered, in an oven preheated at 180°C (350°F) for 35-45 minutes or until rosy and lightly golden, cooked well through and aromatic. (Alternatively cook them hot and fast: 220°C/425°F for 20-25 minutes and serve them far more rare.)

4 Take the whole casserole to the picnic, wrapped first in foil then in a heavy cloth. Serve hot, warm or cool.

tortilla omelette

This is one of the world's most loved, most delicious and most portable of dishes but there are one or two authentic tricks to learn to make sure it emerges perfectly. If you want to cook individual tortillas, sauté the vegetables in a large pan and cook the egg and vegetable mixture in small cast-iron frying pans, about 12.5cm (5 in) in diameter – these will cook more quickly than a large tortilla.

METHOD

1 Heat 4 tablespoons of the oil in a large heavy grill-(broiler-) safe frying pan about 30cm (12 in) in diameter and add the prepared potatoes, onion and red (bell) peppers. Sauté over moderate heat for about 15 minutes, stirring occasionally. Cover the pan and cook for a further 15 minutes or until tender.

2 Using a fork, lightly beat the eggs, salt and pepper in a large bowl. Tip the potato mixture into the beaten eggs.

3 Quickly wash and dry the frying pan and return to the heat, adding the remaining olive oil. When the oil is hot, pour the egg and potato mixture into the frying pan. Cook over high heat for 3–4 minutes, then reduce heat to moderate. Cook the tortilla, undisturbed, for 10–12 minutes until the base is golden and firm. With a fork, pull back the edges of the tortilla and allow the uncooked mixture to run underneath.

4 Preheat the grill (broiler) and cook the top of the tortilla for 2–3 minutes or until it sets firm.

5 Take the tortilla in its pan, divide into wedges and serve.

Note:
Both Fauchon and Hédiard, in Paris, have sold the small cast-iron pans for years, or they are available from specialist kitchen suppliers.

Makes 6

Ingredients

7 tablespoons extra virgin olive oil

500g (1 lb) large potatoes, peeled, quartered and thickly sliced

450g (about 2) Spanish onions, thickly sliced

2 red (bell) peppers, cored, deseeded and diced

8 large fresh free-range eggs

1 teaspoon salt

½ teaspoon freshly ground black pepper

italianate chicken breasts

Serves 8

Ingredients

  8 boneless, skinless chicken breasts (breast halves)
  150g (5 oz) mozzarella, sliced into 16
  100g (4 oz) pecorino or scamorza cheese, sliced into 16
  8 sprigs rosemary or fresh basil, halved
  16 slices garlicky salami, e.g. Milano
  8 slices prosciutto di Parma (cured Italian ham)
  8 garlic cloves, crushed
  4 tablespoons extra virgin olive oil
  fresh flatleaf parsley, to garnish

METHOD

1 Preheat the oven to 200°C (400°F). Make two crosswise cuts, three-quarters of the way through each chicken breast (half), at a slight angle. Push first a slice of mozzarella, then pecorino, then a herb sprig into each slash.

2 Remove any skin from the salami, fold each slice in two, and push one into each cut as well. Continue until each chicken breast cut is evenly filled and all ingredients are used up.

3 Slide a ham slice under each chicken breast, and push a garlic clove between the ham and chicken. Loosely wrap the ham over the chicken.

4 Set the ham-wrapped chicken breasts on a folded sheet of aluminium foil on an oven tray. Drizzle 1$\frac{1}{2}$ teaspoons of oil over each and fold the foil to enclose. Bake in the oven for 20–25 minutes or until cooked through. Refold the foil to enclose and wrap the chicken for transport.

5 Unwrap the foil and serve hot, warm or cool.

field mushroom tart

Serves 8

Ingredients

  4 large, flat field or portobello-type mushrooms
  50g (1 tbsp) garlic and parsley butter
  2 tablespoons extra virgin olive oil
  150ml ($\frac{2}{3}$ cup) single (light) cream
  3 free range eggs, beaten
  375g (13 oz) short pastry, rolled 3mm ($\frac{1}{8}$ in) thick
  1 slice stale bread, processed or grated into crumbs
  small bunch of chives, parsley, oregano or a mixture, chopped

METHOD

1 Remove stalks from mushrooms; trim the stalks and slice thinly. Wipe mushrooms using a damp cloth.

2 Heat butter and oil in a large, non-stick frying pan. Add mushrooms, gill-side downwards, and stalks. Cook 5 minutes, uncovered. Turn them; cover and cook 5 minutes. Preheat oven to 220°C (400°F).

3 Use the pastry to line a 25cm (10 in) fluted, loose-bottomed flan tin, pressing it into the tin. Trim the edges and discard the trimmings. Halve each mushroom and put in the pastry case, gills up, in a decorative pattern; add the sliced stalks.

4 Using a fork, lightly beat the cream and eggs. Pour around mushrooms. Stir the crumbs into the pan to soak up any butter-oil mix. Scatter these over the flan. Bake for about 20 minutes then reduce heat to 180°C (350°F). Cook for a further 15–20 minutes or until the egg is set.

5 To serve, scatter the fresh herbs over the top. Serve in slices or wedges, hot, warm or cool.

baked spiced beef

Serves 8

Ingredients

1kg (2¼ lb) beef fillet, in the piece
2 teaspoons allspice berries
1 tablespoon black peppercorns
1 teaspoon cloves
½ teaspoon ground mace
2 teaspoons coarse salt crystals
2 garlic cloves, crushed to a paste
1 tablespoon vinaigrette
2 tablespoons virgin olive oil

METHOD

1 Tie the beef in four places across with string and push a metal skewer through it, lengthwise.

2 Using a pestle and mortar, pound the spices and salt to a powder. Mix the garlic paste and vinaigrette together. Place the beef in a metal roasting pan, and rub the garlic mixture over. Pat on the spice mixture. Leave to stand 20 minutes or up to 1 hour at room temperature. Preheat the oven to 230ºC (450ºF).

3 Heat the oil in a large non-stick frying pan and brown the meat all over, about 8 minutes. Roast the beef for 26 minutes, no extra. Using a meat thermometer, the internal temperature must be 65ºC (150ºF) or rare, 70ºC (160ºF) for medium rare. The beef should be crusty outside, rosy inside.

4 Leave the meat to stand in its pan for at least 20 minutes. Remove the skewer. If you must refrigerate the beef, but it tastes better cool.

5 Transport the beef whole or carved: serve in 1cm (½ in) slices, hot, warm or cool, with any pan juices. Serve plain or with some horseradish sauce and coarse grain mustard.

herbed potatoes

Serves 8

Ingredients

8 baking potatoes, washed and dried
120g (½ cup) garlic or herb butter
salt and freshly ground black pepper

Topping alternatives:
200ml (1 cup) natural yogurt
or 100g (1 cup) grated Cheddar cheese
or 100g (½ cup) sun-dried tomato paste
or 100g (½ cup) hummus or guacamole
or 100g (½ cup) sauce tartare
handful fresh herbs e.g. parsley, chives, basil, tarragon

METHOD

1 Push a long metal skewer through four potatoes; repeat with the other four. Set them directly on to the top rack of an oven preheated to 220ºC (425ºF). Bake for 1¼-1½ hours or until soft when pressed.

2 Remove the potatoes from the oven and remove the skewer. Make a criss-cross cut on the flat top of each hot potato. Squeeze slightly to open them, and insert about a tablespoon of garlic or herb butter; sprinkle with some salt and pepper. Press on the cuts to close them.

3 Wrap each hot potato first in foil, then kitchen paper, then foil again. This way they'll stay hot for some hours, and undamaged. Take a selection of topping alternatives in sturdy pots with lids. Wrap the herbs in wetted paper, then foil and take along too.

4 To serve, unwrap the potatoes. Squeeze open. Dot on some topping, add fresh herbs and eat.

SALADS

wild rice salad

wild rice salad

Serves 3-4

Ingredients

250g (1²/₃ cups) wild rice, pre-soaked 2 hours if wished
750ml (3 cups) boiling salted water
4 garlic cloves, crushed then chopped
120ml (¹/₂ cup) virgin olive oil vinaigrette
1 bunch spring onions (scallions), shredded
1 handful mâche (lamb's lettuce), dandelion greens
    or watercress
30g (1 oz) fresh herbs, e.g. parsley, mint, basil, chives,
    chervil or a mixture

METHOD

1 Drain the pre-soaked rice or rinse it briefly in cold water. Cover it with the measured boiling salted water. Bring back to a boil, reduce the heat, part-cover and cook for 45–55 minutes or according to the packet instructions. The grains should have 'give' when pressed. Drain the cooked rice.

2 Combine the garlic and the vinaigrette. Stir this well into the rice. Cool slightly. Pack into a snap-top bowl, or use a bowl and cover tightly with plastic wrap.

3 Put the prepared spring onions (scallions) and salad greens of your choice and the herbs into another snap-top bowl or an airtight container such as a plastic bag. If using a bag, puff it up, full of air until it is tight, then secure with an elastic band: this keeps the succulent-textured greens crisp.

4 On site, toss everything together, leaving some of the herbs on top as garnish. Serve.

> Variation
> Add 4 hard-boiled eggs, shelled and halved lengthwise, to top this salad and make it into a full main dish, which can be served on its own.

bacon, rocket & leek salad

Serves 4

Ingredients

2 medium leeks or 12 spring onions (scallions)
3 tablespoons extra virgin olive oil
8 rashers smoked streaky bacon, rind trimmed, chopped
2 tablespoons raspberry or other fruit vinegar
100g (2 large handfuls) fresh rocket (arugula)

METHOD

1 Finely slice the white parts of leek or spring onions (scallions) crosswise. Put into a sieve or colander. Slice the green sections into 5cm (2 in) lengths, rinse well to clean them then slice them lengthwise into julienne strips. Put in a saucepan.

2 Pour boiling water over the green leek or spring onion (scallion) shreds. Bring the pan contents back to boiling point until the leeks turn a brilliant green. Pour pan contents over the shredded white parts. Refresh leeks under cold water. Shake fairly dry. Pack into a salad bowl or a snap-top plastic box.

3 Heat the olive oil in a frying pan and cook the bacon until crisp. Remove it from the pan using a slotted spoon. Allow it to cool and wrap it in foil.

4 Pour the vinegar into the drippings left in the pan and stir to make a dressing. Pour this into a screw-top jar, flask or bottle. Do not chill.

5 Pack the wetted rocket (arugula) on top of the leek. Seal with plastic wrap if using a bowl, or close the lid of the box.

6 On site, toss the leek, bacon and dressing with the rocket (arugula) and serve.

radicchio with red onion salad

Serves 4

Ingredients

2-3 heads radicchio (round, red Italian chicory)
2 red onions, thinly sliced
100g (½ cup) raw broad (fava) beans (optional)
4 tablespoons extra virgin olive oil
2 tablespoons hazelnut oil
2 garlic cloves, crushed
3 tablespoons balsamic vinegar (or 1 if aged)
squeeze of lemon juice (optional)
75g (½ cup) salted, roast hazelnuts, coarsely chopped
sea salt flakes and freshly ground black pepper

METHOD

1 Separate the washed radicchio heads but keep the cup shapes intact. Put the onions into a sieve. Pour some boiling water over them to blanch them then refresh immediately in cold water. Drain.

2 Pack these in a salad bowl, snap-top box or salad spinner. Wrap the beans in a twist of waxed paper and pack with the salad.

3 Combine the oils, garlic, vinegar, lemon juice, nuts and seasoning. Whisk or shake to blend. Take the dressing in a screw-top jar, flask or stoppered bottle.

4 Using salad servers, toss all the components together with the dressing. Serve without too much delay.

rocket & parmesan salad

Serves 4

Ingredients

350g bunch of fresh rocket (arugula)
small bottle estate-bottled cold, first-pressed olive oil
250g (9 oz) Parmesan cheese (Parmigiano Reggiano)

METHOD

1 Take the rocket (arugula) washed, not shaken dry, packed in a snap-top bowl, or a plastic or waxed paper bag

2 Take the little bottle of estate-bottled olive oil. Pack the Parmesan cheese and a potato peeler or sharp knife to cut it in curls or slivers.

3 When ready to eat, toss the rocket (arugula) with the olive oil and add the curls of cheese last.

vinaigrette

Makes about 240ml (1 cup)

Ingredients

2 teaspoons English or Dijon mustard
2 tablespoons wine vinegar or lemon juice
8–12 tablespoons extra virgin olive oil
sea salt flakes and ground black pepper

1 Shake or whisk all the ingredients together using a screw-top jar, a stoppered flask, a shaker or a bowl.

2 Transfer to an appropriate container as necessary to carry to the picnic site.

Variations

Use grainy mustard.
Add any of the following:
2 crushed garlic cloves;
crumbled dried chilli;
1 teaspoon clear honey;
chopped green herbs such as parsley,
   tarragon, chives, rosemary.

salsa verde

Makes about 400ml

Ingredients

- 50g (2oz) tiny pickled capers, drained
- 50g (2 oz) canned or salted anchovies, chopped
- 50g (2 oz) small pickled gherkins (cornichons), chopped
- 1 tablespoon gherkin pickling liquid
- 4 garlic cloves, crushed and chopped
- 2 teaspoons pickled or dried green peppercorns, crushed
- juice of 1 lemon (3 tablespoons)
- ½ teaspoon finely shredded lemon zest (optional)
- 1 handful fresh basil, parsley, lovage, oregano or marjoram, chopped
- 6-8 tablespoons extra virgin olive oil
- 2 tablespoons fresh breadcrumbs

1 Combine the first 6 ingredients in a mortar or food processor. Pound using a pestle or process briefly in bursts to mash and amalgamate the ingredients.

2 Add the remaining ingredients, stirring to mix. Refrigerate and serve within 2 days.

3 Serve at room temperature as a sauce for chicken, fish, grills etc.

mayonnaise

Makes 450-500ml (1½ cups)

Ingredients

- 1 egg, at room temperature
- 2 egg yolks, at room temperature
- 2 teaspoons Dijon mustard
- 1 tablespoon wine vinegar
- ½ teaspoon salt
- ½ teaspoon freshly ground black pepper
- 200ml (scant 1 cup) extra virgin olive oil
- 200ml (scant 1 cup) grapeseed oil
- 2 tablespoons boiling water

1 Combine the first 6 ingredients in a food processor. Process in a brief burst to mix.

2 Mix the oils together, and, using a measuring jug, drizzle in the oils with the motor running. Gradually increase the trickle to a slow, steady pour until the mayonnaise thickens to a dense emulsion. Stop the machine now and then to scrape down the mixture from the sides.

3 Add the boiling water in a slow drizzle. Transfer the finished mayonnaise to an airtight container. Cool. This will keep, refrigerated, for up to 1 week.

4 Spoon out into a bowl or portable container. Keep cool and use the same day. It tastes best eaten at room temperature.

Variations
Aioli
Add 4 crushed chopped garlic cloves to the first lot of ingredients.

Seafood Mayonnaise
Add 2 tablespoons of tomato passata, ¼ teaspoon anchovy sauce or paste and several shakes of Tabasco sauce to the mix before adding boiling water.

Note:

As this mayonnaise contains raw egg, do not serve to young children, or to anyone who is sick, elderly or pregnant.

nuoc cham

Makes 125ml (½ cup)

Ingredients

- 4 tablespoons rice vinegar or fresh lime juice
- 2 teaspoons clear honey or palm sugar
- 4 tablespoons chicken or vegetable stock
- 1 teaspoon dark sesame oil, or more to taste
- 2 tablespoons fish sauce
- 1-2 fresh birds' eye chillies, sliced
- 1-2 teaspoons toasted sesame seeds (optional)

1 Stir or shake together all the ingredients in a non-reactive bowl, screw-topped jar or stoppered flask until the honey or sugar is fully dissolved. Refrigerate for up to 1 week.

2 Shake again; serve cool or chilled in tiny, individual dishes or a bowl with a ladle.

Variations
Add 1 kaffir lime leaf, sliced in hair-like shreds.
Add 2 tablespoons chopped Vietnamese mint, Chinese chives or Thai holy basil.
Omit the sesame seeds and substitute finely chopped salted, roasted peanuts.

pashka with fruits

DESSERTS & DRINKS

pashka with fruits

Traditionally these little Russian puddings came as part of a spring celebration: a profusion of dairy products and dried fruits being some of the original features. But make them at any time, any season. Use one large bowl or several small 'timbale' moulds or even small glass tumblers. With the help of a strip of foil, each pudding is easily removed at serving time and the shapes stay perfect.

METHOD

1 Combine all the ingredients in a large bowl or a food processor. Stir energetically to mix or process, in brief bursts, in the food processor until the mix is uniform in consistency. Taste. Add extra honey if needed.

2 Cut 8 strips of aluminium foil about 12 x 4cm (1½ x 4½ in) in size. Fold in half lengthwise, twice. Press the strips into 8 small, metal 'timbale' moulds (about 100ml/scant ½ cup in volume) so the strips lie smoothly across the base and up the sides. Leave the excess to use as 'handles'.

3 Spoon in the pashka mixture and press it down well. Chill for several hours or overnight.

4 Transport to the site in the moulds. Invert each pudding, and pull the foil strip downwards, unmoulding each one on to a plate. To serve, pour a pool of liqueur round each tower-shaped pudding.

Serves 8

Ingredients

400g (2 cups) full-fat cream cheese
250g (1 cup) curd cheese, quark or low fat soft cheese
4 tablespoons citrus liqueur e.g. Limoncello or Mandarine, plus extra to decorate
6-8 tablespoons clear honey
75g (1½ cups) fresh yellow cake crumbs
½ teaspoon orange flower water
2 teaspoons grated orange zest
75g (½ cup) chopped mixed peel
75g (¾ cup) flaked almonds

macadamia, lime & white chocolate cookies

Though these cookies need careful handing when newly cooked, crumbly and still warm, they are easy to make and have a subtle flavour. The salted nuts help balance the sweetness of the dough and the richness of the chocolate. Decorate them however you like.

METHOD

1 Toast the nuts in a preheated oven at 160-170°C (325-340°C) for 15-20 minutes or so until they are dry, hot but not browned. Cool. Hand chop 50g (2 oz) of them coarsely and set aside. Using a food processor in brief bursts, chop the remainder to a coarse meal.

2 Cream the butter and sugar until pale and light. Stir in the nut 'meal', the zest and juice, then the flour. Mix, then knead in the bowl to make the dough into a dense, soft ball.

3 Roll it out between two sheets of plastic wrap to about 3mm (1 in) thickness. Use shaped cutters to cut out 24-32 shapes, each about 5-7cm (2-3 in) diameter. Re-roll any left-over dough and use this for more shapes.

4 Carefully transfer the dough shapes to 2 large baking trays ideally lined with non-stick paper, setting them about 2cm (³/₄ in) apart. Adjust oven temperature to 150°C (300°F) and bake for 20-23 minutes or until pale golden, crisp but pliable. Remove the trays. Let them stand for 10 minutes then transfer the cookies to wire racks to cool.

5 Heat the white chocolate and cream over boiling water until melted. Stir until smooth. Use to paint, dip or drizzle chocolate over to decorate.

6 Push on the reserved chopped macadamia nuts. Cool until cold and set. Store in an airtight container, between layers of greaseproof paper, until ready to serve and eat.

Makes 24-32

Ingredients

300g (11 oz) salted macadamia nuts
250g (1 cup) spreadable butter
125g (generous ¹/₂ cup) vanilla sugar
2 teaspoons fresh lime zest, shredded
2 tablespoons freshly squeezed lime juice
300g (2³/₄ cups) self-raising flour
150g (5 oz) white chocolate, broken
3 tablespoons single (light) cream

angel cake with citrus frosting

Angel cake, or Angel Food Cake, is made without any egg yolks so it is white, fluffy and so ephemeral that it really does deserve its name. Vanilla, almond and citrus flavours are a feature of this indulgent offering with its generous frosting. Transport this special cake carefully, and decorate with green grapes, citrus slices or wild flowers if you like.

METHOD

1 Have ready a large, deep ring-shaped cake tin with removable base (angel-cake tin). Do not grease or flour it.

2 Combine egg whites, salt with and cream of tartar in a large bowl. Whisk continuously until the mix stands up in soft peaks. Set aside 50g ($\frac{1}{4}$ cup) caster sugar; gradually add the remaining caster sugar, whisking continuously.

3 Mix the reserved caster sugar with the flour. Fold this mixture into the whisked whites gently and firmly. Stir in the essence and smooth it gently through the cake batter.

4 Smooth this batter into the cake tin. Bake at the centre of an oven preheated to 190°C (375°F) for 28-30 minutes. Reduce the heat to 275°C (190°F) and continue to cook for 16-18 minutes. Test the cake: it should feel slightly springy to the touch and be shrinking a little from the edges.

5 Remove from the oven and let it stand for 10 minutes; run a knife around the edges of the cake. Put a rack on top. Invert both quickly and cool the turned-out cake on a rack.

6 Beat the frosting ingredients together using a minimal amount of juice – it must not become too soft. Frost the cake all over and transport it in a snap-top plastic or metal cake box, setting the cake on the lid and closing it by pushing the base on to it from above. Keep the box this way up.

7 Undo the box on the spot, when you are ready to eat, and decorate as you like.

Serves 8

Ingredients

Angel Cake:
   7 egg whites, at room temperature
   pinch of salt
   $\frac{1}{2}$ teaspoon cream of tartar
   225g ($1\frac{1}{4}$ cups) caster sugar
   75g ($\frac{3}{4}$ cup) plain flour or cake flour, sifted
   1 teaspoon almond essence

Frosting:
   450g (2 cups) cream cheese
   100g ($\frac{3}{4}$ cup) icing sugar, sifted
   shredded zest of 2 limes and a little juice
   $\frac{1}{4}$-$\frac{1}{2}$ teaspoon almond essence

Note:
If the day is very hot, try to keep the cake cool and fresh. Do not freeze it. Both cake and frosting can, however, be made, and chilled, in their containers, a day in advance.

smoothies, crushes & variations

Although these can be bought, ready-made, your own combinations are freshest and best. Vary these according to the fruits available. Use a half-cup measure or a wine glass as your volume measure and the unit constant. You'll also need a large and sturdy blender.

pineapple-honey-citrus smoothie

Each drink serves 4

Ingredients
2 parts natural yogurt, ideally live
2 parts cubed fresh pineapple
2 parts freshly squeezed orange or grapefruit juice
½ part clear honey
1 part ice cubes

METHOD

1 Combine the first 4 ingredients in a blender. Blend. Add the ice and blend again until the ice is no longer visible and the drink is a thickish liquid. Add a little water if liked, to thin it slightly.

2 If made ahead, store it in a vacuum flask but take extra ice and shake the smoothie well to chill it again before serving, or pour it over the ice in the glasses or containers. Serve with thick drinking straws.

Variations
raspberry-pineapple

Make as before adding 2 parts fresh or thawed raspberries and use orange, not grapefruit juice. Blend these first 5 ingredients and then the ice.

plum, banana and blackberry

2 parts natural yogurt, ideally live
1 part fresh or thawed blackberries
1 part cubed, red-fleshed plums
1 part chopped banana
2 parts freshly squeezed blood orange or orange juice
½ part clear honey
1 part ice cubes
Make as before, blending the first 6 ingredients,
    then the ice cubes.

mango, raspberry and orange crush

2 parts cubed fresh mango
1 part chopped banana
¼ part fresh or thawed raspberries
2 parts freshly squeezed orange juice
1 part ice cubes
Make as before, blending the first 4 ingredients,
    then the ice cubes.

home-made ginger beer fizz

Makes 8 litres (2 gallons)

Ingredients

2 teaspoons dried yeast granules
900g (3 cups) granulated sugar
2 tablespoons ground ginger
1 tablespoon lemonade, undiluted
   (see right) or ½ teaspoon lemon oil
2 teaspoons tartaric acid
950ml (4 cups) hot water
5 litres (10½ pints) cold water
To serve: Ice, sliced lemon; straws

METHOD

1 Stir yeast with 60ml (¼ cup) warm water and 1 teaspoon of the sugar. Put remaining sugar, ginger, cordial and tartaric acid into a plastic bucket. Stir in the hot water until sugar is dissolved. Add the cold water. Whisk in yeast mix.

2 Using a funnel, pour ginger beer into 8 flexible plastic bottles. Pour boiling water over the tops, and drain them. Pinch the shoulders of the bottle to allow for expansion then screw on the tops.

3 Leave the bottles at room temperature for at least 4-6 days. During this time the pressure will increase: test one bottle; when the beer tastes slightly fizzy, refrigerate them all.

4 Try to avoid shaking the bottles. Serve over ice with lemon and drinking straws.

home-made lemonade & soda

Serves 6-8

Ingredients

400ml (scant 1 cup) water
400g (1 cup) sugar
zest, and juice of 8 lemons
3 teaspoons citric acid
½ teaspoon Epsom salts
   (magnesium sulphate)
zest of 1 orange, in fine shreds
3 litres (6½ pints) sparkling water
   or soda to dilute
ice, to serve
drinking straws (optional)

METHOD

1 Boil the water and sugar to make a syrup. Add lemon juice and stir well; add the citric acid and Epsom salts. Add the citrus zest, stir well and remove from the heat. Allow to stand for 2 minutes. Strain well. Cool the syrup over ice. Pour it into a vacuum flask or stoppered jug.

2 Take sparkling water or soda. Take ice cubes in an insulated container. Dilute about 1 part cordial to 3-4 parts sparkling water and serve with some ice cubes, and straws if you like.

Note:
Fresh herbs such as lovage, mint or lemon balm may be added as a decoration. So can slices of citrus fruits of your choice.

home-made limeade

Serves 4

Ingredients

5 fresh limes, 1 with zest removed
   in 4 long strips
4 tablespoons vanilla or caster sugar
iced soda water, to top up
ice cubes or crushed ice, to top up

METHOD

1 'Muddle' or mash up one strip of lime in each of the bases of 4 tall glasses with its share of sugar. Squeeze all the limes. Divide this juice between the glasses. Stir them again until the sugar is dissolved.

2 Heap in some ice: half-fill each glass. Top up with soda water. Stir. Serve with drinking straws.

Variations
Bitter Limeade Shake in some Peychaud bitters, Angostura bitters or orange bitters. Stir.
Chilli Limeade In India this is sometimes called *nimbu pani*. Omit the sugar. Add a whole fresh chilli to each glass, pushed on to a satay or cocktail stick, and a sprinkle of salt in place of the sugar.
Kaffir Limeade Add 1 fresh kaffir lime leaf (washed and crushed) to each drink at the end of mixing. Stir. (Substitute lemon-scented verbena as an alternative.)

SUPPLIERS

For accessories such as plates, napkins and containers:

The Conran Shop
Michelin House
81 Fulham Road
London SW3 6RD
Tel: 020 7589 7401

Habitat
Branches throughout the UK
Tel: 0845 601 0740

Harvey Nichols
109-125 Knightsbridge
London SW1X 7RJ
Tel: 020 7235 5000
www.harveynichols.com

Heal's
196 Tottenham Court Road
London W1P 9LD
Tel: 020 7636 1666
www.heals.com

Ikea
2 Drury Way
North Circular Road
London NW10 0TH
Tel: 020 8208 5600
Branches throughout the UK

John Lewis Partnership
Oxford Street
London W1A 1EX
Tel: 020 7629 7711
Branches throughout the UK

Liberty
210-220 Regent Street
London W1
Tel: 020 7734 1234
www.liberty.co.uk

Muji
6-17 Tottenham Court Road
London W1P 9DP
and branches
Tel: for stockists 020 8323 2208
www.muji.co.jp

Purves & Purves
80-81 & 83 Tottenham Court Road
London W1
Tel: 020 7580 8223
www.purves.co.uk

Selfridges & Co
400 Oxford Street
London W1A 1AB

For rugs and other decorative items:

Designers Guild
267 Kings Road
London SW3 5EN
Tel: 020 7351 5775
www.designersguild.com

Earth Tones
36 Trent Avenue
London W5 4TL
Tel: 020 7221 9300
www.earthtones.co.uk

Egg
36 Kinnerton Street
London SW1
Tel: 020 7235 9315

Liberty, *as above*

Selfridges, *as above*

Supermarkets during the summer often stock very good items for your essential kit.

For delicious delicacies to pop into your picnic basket, try:

Borough Market
8 Southwark Street
London SE1
Tel: 020 7407 1002
www.boroughmarket.org.uk
Opening hours: Friday 12 noon - 6pm
Saturday 9am - 4pm

Divertimenti
33-34 Marylebone High Street
London W1U 4PT
www.divertimenti.co.uk

The Grocer on Elgin
6 Elgin Crescent
London W11 2HX
Tel: 020 7221 3844
www.thegroceron.com

Rias Atlas Delicatessen
97 Frampton Street
London NW8 8NA
Tel: 020 7262 434

ACKNOWLEDGEMENTS

The publisher wishes to thank Rhona Nuttall and Kathryn Dighton at Muji for all the items they loaned for photography. Muji's containers are superbly practical, they withstand wear and tear and - above all - are aesthetically beautiful as well as functional. To Earth Tones, many thanks for all the divine rugs and throws that were supplied which even kept the crew warm on a few gale-force days.

Also we would like to thank John Lewis Partnership, YHA Adventure Shops and Habitat for their help.

AUTHOR'S ACKNOWLEDGEMENTS

Thanks to Bethany Heald, assistant food stylist, recipe tester and editorial assistant, and to Christine Boodle of Better Read Limited for her word-processing skills. The following food and wine suppliers and specialist shops have helped immeasurably in the evolution of this book:

Chalmers and Gray, Fishmongers, of Notting Hill Gate, London W11

R. Garcia and Sons, Spanish Delicatessen, of Portobello Road, London W11

Jeroboams Cheese and Wine, of Holland Park Avenue, London W11

David Lidgate of C. Lidgate, Butchers and Charcutiers, of Holland Park Avenue, London W11

Speck, Italian Delicatessen, of Portland Road, Holland Park, London W11

Michanicou Brothers, Greengrocers, of Clarendon Road, London W11

Mr Christian's Delicatessen, of Elgin Crescent, Notting Hill, London W11

Kingsland, The Edwardian Butchers, of Portobello Road, London W11

Portobello Road stallholders and shopkeepers, of London W11, whose vivacity is a constant inspiration.